Calder-isms

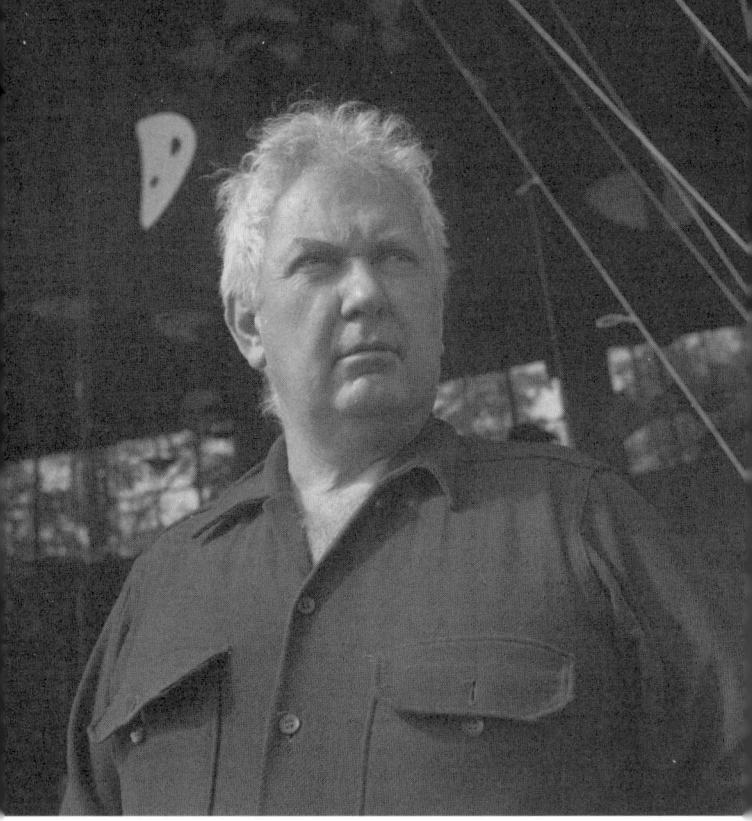

Calder-isms

Alexander Calder

Edited by Larry Warsh

PRINCETON UNIVERSITY PRESS

Princeton and Oxford

in association with

No More Rulers

Princeton University Press is committed to the protection of copyright and the intellectual property our authors entrust to us. Copyright promotes the progress and integrity of knowledge created by humans. By engaging with an authorized copy of this work, you are supporting creators and the global exchange of ideas. As this work is protected by copyright, any reproduction or distribution of it in any form for any purpose requires permission; permission requests should be sent to permissions@press.princeton.edu. Ingestion of any PUP IP for any AI purposes is strictly prohibited.

Published by Princeton University Press,
41 William Street, Princeton, New Jersey 08540

In the United Kingdom: Princeton University Press,
99 Banbury Road, Oxford OX2 6JX
GPSR Authorized Representative: Easy Access System Europe -
Mustamäe tee 50, 10621 Tallinn, Estonia,
gpsr.requests@easproject.com

press.princeton.edu
in association with
No More Rulers
nomorerulers.com
ISMs is a trademark of No More Rulers, Inc.

P PRINCETON   NO MORE RULERS ®

All Rights Reserved

ISBN 978-0-691-27511-6
Library of Congress Control Number: 2025936043

British Library Cataloging-in-Publication Data is available
This book has been composed in Joanna MT
Printed in China

1 3 5 7 9 10 8 6 4 2

CONTENTS

INTRODUCTION

Alexander Calder revolutionized how we experience art in space. A trailblazer in the world of sculpture and inventor of the "mobile," he challenged traditional boundaries in art, composing not only with color and form but with balance, movement, and the unpredictability of external forces. Much like his life, Calder's art was dynamic, unconventional, and filled with vitality—a quality that resonates in his words as in his artwork. Energetic and elegant, his work has no utility but beauty. For Calder, art is meant not only to engage the senses but to ignite the spirit.

As fate determines so many of our paths, Calder fell into being an artist. Born into a family of artists, he was sculpting in clay by the age of three. Unlike most of us, he never lost that intuitive ability to see the world through a lens of wonder, curiosity, and endless possibility. *Cirque Calder*, a complex piece of performance art, is one wonderful example. Calder's collection of handmade wire figures and circus acts, from acrobatics to lion taming, was embraced by the international avant-garde in 1920s Paris and New York. As a vehicle for Calder's legendary performances, and as an ensemble sculpture in its own right, Calder's miniature circus was a profound artistic statement filled with spontaneity and depth.

The first truly international artist, Calder traveled frequently and surrounded himself with the brightest minds in the art world. Artists such as Marcel Duchamp, Fernand Léger, Jean Arp, Piet Mondrian, and Joan Miró were friends. While these experiences enriched his imaginative life, he retained an unyielding commitment to his own vision, constantly experimenting. Working in multiple mediums, he was a master of materials. He had a conscious indifference to how his work was regarded, allowing his sense of freedom to guide his creativity. He didn't explain his work or imbue it with meaning but rather encouraged his viewers to have unmediated experiences. With the wisdom of a philosopher and the ingenuity of a true original, Calder reinvented what it meant to be an artist.

Calder-isms invites readers to step into his remarkable world, offering a glimpse into the mind of this extraordinary artist and individual. Taken from primary sources such as interviews, writings, and artist statements, the quotes in this book distill Calder's unique outlook on art, creativity, process, and existence. Much like his mobiles, which respond to the currents of air and shifting environments around them, Calder's thoughts and experiences encourage us to embrace change, experiment freely, and value the unexpected.

LARRY WARSH

MARCH 2025

Calder-isms

Beginnings

I always thought I was born—at least my mother always told me so—on August 22, 1898. But my grandfather Milne's birthday was on August 23, so there might have been a little confusion. (32)

———

In 1942, when I wrote the Philadelphia City Hall for a birth certificate, I sent them a dollar and they told me I was born on the twenty-second of July, 1898. So I sent them another dollar and told them, "Look again." They corroborated the first statement. (32)

———

I wasn't brought up—I was framed. (4)

———

My father was a sculptor and my mother a painter, but it was quite accidentally that I became mixed up with modern art. (6)

———

My Scottish grandfather was a stonecutter. He worked in London, then in America. My father was a sculptor. I never worked for him, except to pose for him. (23)

———

In Philadelphia, when I was four, father made the "Man Cub," for which I posed. I remember his studio over an old livery stable, two flights up. I liked it because the door opened with a long chain. … At that time I believe I did a clay elephant. (32)

———

Later in San Francisco I posed for my mother too; she painted several portraits, and it was sort of a bore. (32)

———

My sister Peggy was born two years before me, in Paris, during a stay of my parents. Her being born in Paris I found exciting. Mother used to call her "Peggy from Paris" and wished she had red hair and played the violin. Mother was disappointed on either count, but Peggy was a good girl. (32)

———

When I was a kid, I had many toys, but I was never satisfied with them. I always embellished and expanded their repertoire with additions made of steel wire, copper, and other materials. (11)

———

On Euclid Avenue in Pasadena [in 1906], I got my first tools and was given the cellar with its window as a workshop. Mother and father were all for my efforts to build things myself—they approved of the home-made. I used to make all sorts of things, little seats, or a tonneau cover for my coaster wagon. (33)

———

My workshop became some sort of a center of attraction; everybody came in. Peggy once gave me a very nice pair of pliers at Christmas. I made her a little Christmas tree, completely decorated, out of a fallen branch. (33)

———

I had a friend with whom I made armor and weapons from tin and wood, shields, breastplates, helmets, swords, lances; I even covered an old pair of my mother's gloves in tin scales. He was Sir Lancelot, and I was Sir Tristan. (11)

———

My sister had quite a few dolls, and using very fine copper wire we found in the street after electric cables were spliced, and beads, we made extraordinary jewelry. (11)

———

[In Croton-on-Hudson], too, I had a cellar workshop. I think I was respected by my playmates for what I could make out of wood and leather with my tools and hands. One time I even made an electric light plug out of a cork, a nail, and a piece of copper wire. But after drawing an enormous spark from this apparatus, I quit bothering electricity. (46)

———

Father's skylight [at the Panama-Pacific International Exposition] was located in some very large iron workshop erected on the fair grounds. I often went to visit him and was very much interested in the pointing machine for enlarging small sculpture. … I'd be particularly fascinated by the mechanics, the rotating motions and the parallel needles of the process. (34)

––––

It was father who suggested that I try to join [Clinton Balmer's] course and draw under him. I became very enthusiastic—more so than in any other of my post-college ventures so far—and attended consistently. (47)

––––

I don't remember much of Clinton Balmer's instructions; he was a pleasant and mild man. But I remember that when you wanted to draw a new line, he asked you to draw a shadow over the old line—we crosshatched it. I still do that now when working on a stabile or other model. (47)

———

When there is some particularly dramatic effect of nature I am always willing to stay up for that—and I remember [in 1922] a very beautiful hot red sunrise off Guatemala with a pale tin moon on the opposite side, a deep blue sky, and the sea all about us. (7)

———

It was early one morning on a calm sea, off Guatemala, when over my couch—a coil of rope—I saw the beginning of a fiery red sunrise on one side and the moon looking like a silver coin on the other. Of the whole trip this impressed me most of all; it left me with a lasting sensation of the solar system. (40)

———

When I was working in a logging camp
I first started painting. (6)

I happened to be in the State of Washington,
working as a [timekeeper]. I wrote to my
mother for her to send me colors: my mother
was a painter herself. Around the forest, there
were three mountains. I put them on my first
canvas. That was how everything began. (21)

Somehow the desire to paint the logging-
camp landscape made me write home
and ask for paints and brushes. (35)

Through some business connection, father had known a certain Canadian engineer. ... He advised me to do what I really wanted to do—he himself often wished he had been an architect. So, I decided to become a painter. (36)

I began by futuristic painting in a small studio in the Greenwich Village section of New York. It was a lot different to engineering but I took to my newfound art immediately. (26)

It was in September–October 1923, at
twenty-five, that I entered the Art Students
League, in New York at Fifty-Seventh Street
near Columbus Circle. ... Mother was
certainly pleased to see me
and father was too. (36)

———

When I went to the Art Students League
I was too old + formed in way of thinking
to be trapped by any system of "art" proposed
to me, unless I really found it good.
Of course I wasn't aware of this—but
it seems clear now. (4)

———

My chief delight [at the Art Students League] was probably hanging up the canvas with a few nails and string. Thus I could attach it to a fence, a post, or anything. I guess the center of my composition was usually a derrick or some such device, and I tried to carve out its most potent features from the surrounding atmosphere. (36)

———

They used to sell wrapping paper at the League and we found out that it was pretty good for drawing. You folded a sheet into eight rectangles and it would fit in your pocket. With this we used to pass our time drawing people in the subway on our way to and fro. I seemed to have a knack for doing it with a single line. (36)

———

[Boardman Robinson] was an excellent
teacher. I guess it was he who taught me to
draw with a pen and a single line. He was a
real person, a big red-headed guy with a
beard. I liked him very much. (36)

———

I also went in the evening to John Sloan's
class. ... Sloan was a good instructor, not
trying to make you do it his way but urging
you to develop some capabilities
of your own. (36)

———

In one of my job-hunting moments, I tried the [National] *Police Gazette*. The editor, Robinson, was interested in this single-line drawing and gave me a modest job, doing half-pages of boxers training, which developed into covering other sports as well. (36)

———

I went to the circus, Ringling Brothers and Barnum & Bailey. I spent two full weeks there practically every day and night. I could tell by the music what act was getting on and used to rush to some vantage point. Some acts were better seen from above and others from below. (37)

———

I was very fond of the spatial relations. I love the space of the circus. I made some drawings of nothing but the tent. The whole thing of the—the vast space—I've always loved it. (16)

There's another thing I like. That's the spotlight that concentrates on a certain area of the circus. (16)

It's just like a diagram of force. I love the mechanics of the [circus]—and the vast space—and the spotlight. (16)

Animals—Action. These two words go hand in hand in art. Our interest in animals is connected with their habits, their food, the animals they prey upon or that prey on them, their habitats and protective coloring. Their lives are of necessity active and their activities are reflected in an alert grace of line even when they are in repose or asleep. ... There is always a feeling of perpetual motion about animals and to draw them successfully this must be borne in mind. (19)

———

[In New York in 1926] I made a sundial
with a piece of wire—a wire rooster on a
vertical rod with radiating lines at the foot
indicating the hours. I'd made things
out of wire before—jewelry, toys—but
this was my first effort to represent
an animal in wire. (36)

———

Paris seemed the place to go, on all accounts
of practically everyone who had been there,
and I decided I would also like to go. My
parents were favorable to this idea. (37)

———

[H]ere in Paris, it's a compliment
to be called crazy. (74)

———

I don't think I wasted much time before
I went to the [Académie de la] Grande
Chaumière to draw. Here there were no
teachers, just a nude model, and everyone was
drawing by himself; the atmosphere was more
subdued than at the Art Students League. (48)

———

I soon was making small animals in wood
and wire and articulating them. I had made
myself a little workbench and bought a few
tools, some steel wire, and some soft
wire in a hardware store on the
avenue d'Orléans. (48)

———

Motives and Motions

Did you have any particular direction or
were you just testing out things?
Well, I didn't think about it.
Every direction was forward. (15)

———

[In Paris in 1926] I made up my mind
to create an entire circus. (11)

———

I made a circus with elephants, horses, a lion,
Roman chariots and so on: basically of wire,
but with cork and wood and bright colors
added. Most of these objects also were articulated, so that they made characteristic gestures.
The material for this was based on my obser-
vation at the circus, and on drawings of it.
I was always interested in circuses. (6)

———

My first acrobat was a tumbler who had legs of steel wire, hands of lead, a body covered in yellow velvet and a head made from a piece of cork with hair and a moustache painted on in gouache. I would let him fall onto his feet, and after many tries and some luck, he would land on his hands. I thought him very successful when a friend of mine said that he looked like her father. (11)

———

I started the circus for myself. An American woman, Frances Robbins, saw it, then she sent an English woman, Mary Butts, who sent Cocteau. He was excited. He started making masks out of pipe cleaners, but they were sort of soft. (16)

———

In all there are about twenty acts with an intermission, peanuts, and exotic gramophone music played by my wife, who is an excellent conductor, and with the sounds of a tambourine, cymbals and a cardboard pipe for making the lion roar and if you like the big circus, then maybe you'll like mine. (11)

———

It was always a long job packing things afterward—like in the real circus—and I always did it myself, having the knack and the memory. (58)

———

I don't think the Circus was really important
in the making of the mobiles. (13)

———

At the same time [as the circus] I began
trying figures wholly in wire, and at
that time made 2 or 3. (1)

———

I did not consider [wire sculpture] to be
of any signal importance in the world of art;
merely a very amusing stunt cleverly executed.
So I began to carve wood. ... However,
wishing to return to Paris, I felt it would be
quite justifiable to have an exhibition here,
where "clever stunts" are highly appreciated,
so I came over ... and set to work, carving
wood and twisting wire. (1)

———

I was a "wire sculptor" as I put it, also "le roi du fil de fer" [the king of wire]. (4)

———

Before, the wire studies were subjective, portraits, caricatures, stylized representations of beasts and humans. But these recent things [from 1929] have been viewed from a more objective angle and although their present size is diminutive, I feel that there is no limitation to the scale to which they can be enlarged. (1)

———

Wire was the principle means of support and propulsion in my abstract work. (66)

———

Father told me once that he was amused
by the small wire things, but that my objects
were too sharp to be caressed and fondled
as one could do with small bronzes. However,
I observed a few years later, with an object
I had just painted black and placed on a
mantelpiece, that somebody took the trouble
to caress it and got full of paint. (38)

———

The "wire sculpture" and the wood sculpture
came to me rather naturally, but the impulse
to work in an abstract manner came to me
through living among, and knowing, those
who were working in that field. (29)

———

It was more or less directly as a result of my visit to Piet Mondrian's studio in 1930, and the sight of all his rectangles of color deployed on the wall, that my first work in the abstract was based on the concept of stellar relationships. Since then there have been variations from this theme, but I always seem to come back to it, in some form or other. For though the lightness of a pierced or serrated solid or surface is extremely interesting the still greater lack of weight of deployed nuclei is much more so. I say nuclei, for to me whatever sphere, or other form, I use in these constructions does not necessarily mean a body of that size, shape or color, but may mean a more minute system of bodies, an atmospheric condition, or even a void. I.E. the idea that one can compose <u>any things</u> of which he can conceive. (9)

I was very much moved by Mondrian's studio, large, beautiful and irregular in shape as it was, with the walls painted white and divided by black lines and rectangles of bright color, like his paintings. It was very lovely, with a cross-light (there were windows on both sides), and I thought at the time how fine it would be if everything there *moved*. (6)

———

It was hard to see the "art" because everything partook of the art. Even the victrola had been painted so as to be in harmony. I must have missed a lot, because it was all one big decor, and the things in the foreground were lost against the things behind. But behind all was the wall running from one window to the other and at a certain spot Mondrian had tacked on it rectangles of the primary colors, and black, gray, + white. In fact there were several whites, some shiny some matte. This caught my attention, and somehow I thought it would be nice if these rectangles oscillated—not much, but a little. (7)

I suggested to Mondrian that perhaps it
would be fun to make these rectangles
oscillate. And he, with a very serious counte-
nance, said: "No, it is not necessary,
my painting is already very fast." (39)

———

This one visit gave me a shock that
started things. Though I had heard the word
"modern" before, I did not consciously
know or feel the term "abstract." (39)

———

That visit to Mondrian gave me the shock
that converted me. It was like the baby being
slapped to make his lungs start working. (7)

———

[It] gave me a shock. A bigger shock, even,
than eight years earlier, when off Guatemala
I saw the beginning of a fiery red sunrise
on one side and the moon looking like a
silver coin on the other. (39)

———

I was much impressed by the simplicity and exactitude [of Mondrian's studio], and I went home and for 2 weeks I tried to paint. But I guess my motto might be, "When there's wire there's a way," for at the end of that period I was again a "wire sculptor"— but this time abstract. (7)

———

It was Mondrian who made me abstract—but I tried to paint, and it was my love of making <u>plastic</u> <u>things</u> that turned me to constructions. From there on it has been the possibility of inventing new mechanical combinations that lend themselves to "my art." (4)

———

Wherever there is a main issue the elimination of other things which are not essential will make for a stronger result. In the earlier static abstract sculptures I was most interested in space, vectoral quantities, and centers of differing densities. (5)

———

The circular forms, particularly interacting, seem to me to have some kind of cosmic or universal feeling. (72)

———

At first I made very simple, static constructions of wire or rod, with elements of wood, tin, brass, attached. And Jean Hélion came to see me, and approved, and I joined the group Abstraction-Création. And I had an exhibition at the Galerie Percier. (7)

———

The idea of making mobiles came to me little by little. I worked with whatever I had at hand. (23)

———

When I was making the objects Arp later called "stabiles" I felt that perhaps I was exactly a perfectionist: i.e. that who was I to decide that a thing should be just this way, or just that way—so I made one or 2 objects articulated, so that they could be in a number of positions. It was this idea that led to the motion, and only a little later that I went after it for the motion itself. (4)

———

Each element able to move, to stir, to oscillate, to come and go in its relationships with the other elements in its universe. It must not be just a "fleeting" moment, but a physical bond between the varying events in life. (2)

———

At first the objects were static ("stabiles"),
seeking to give a sense of cosmic relationship.
Then I felt that these relations were possibly
not the most important and I introduced
flexibility, so that the relationships would
be more general. From that I went to the use
of motion for its contrapuntal value,
as in good choreography. (8)

———

The sense of motion in painting and sculpture has long been considered as one of the primary elements of the composition. The Futurists prescribed for its rendition. (5)

———

When I began to make mobiles, everyone was talking about movement in painting and sculpture. In reality, there wasn't much movement, only actions. (23)

———

Why must art be static? You look at an abstraction, sculptured or painted, an intensely exciting arrangement of planes, spheres, nuclei, entirely without meaning. It would be perfect, but it is always still. The next step in sculpture is motion. (28)

———

I don't think [Duchamp] liked the Circus—
I don't think so. But he liked the other
things I was making. (25)

———

One evening, [Mary Reynolds] brought
Marcel Duchamp to the rue de la Colonie
[studio], to see us and my work. There was
one motor-driven thing, with three elements.
The thing had just been painted and was not
quite dry yet. Marcel said: "Do you mind?"
When he put his hands on it, the object
seemed to please him, so he arranged for me
to show in Marie Cuttoli's Galerie Vignon. ...
I asked him what sort of a name I could
give these things and he at once produced
"Mobile." In addition to something that
moves, in French it also means motive. (42)

———

Duchamp also suggested that on my invitation card I make a drawing of the motor-driven object and print: *Calder: ses mobiles*. (42)

———

Arp said at the time of my mobile show in 1932 at the Galerie Vignon, "Well, if these are mobiles, what do you call those things you had in the show last year [1931, Galerie Percier]—were they stabiles?" So I took that term too. (25)

———

Duchamp named the mobiles and Arp the stabiles. (13)

———

The journalists did not seem to understand anything I was driving at. There were notes about "l'art automobile," and a photograph of one object, likening it to a gear shift. They just did not, or would not, understand. (43)

———

[A mobile] has no utility and no meaning. It is simply beautiful. It has a great emotional effect if you understand it. Of course if it meant anything it would be easier to understand, but it would not be worthwhile. (28)

———

Some critics say that [a motorized mobile] is not sculpture, because in order to appreciate its beauties you have to turn on an electric switch. Well, that is true of any sort of plastic art at night. You have to turn on an electric switch to see it. (28)

―――

As truly serious art must follow the greater laws, and not only appearances, I try to put all the elements in motion in my mobile sculptures. It is a matter of harmonizing these movements, thus arriving at a new possibility of beauty. (3)

―――

The idea of one body moving about
another body which is doing something else,
all by itself, is very exciting to me. And I think
I have remained faithful to this original
conception—that disparity is the spice of life,
i.e. disparity of form, size density color and
motion and perhaps a few other things.
At all events I became interested in
composing motions. In essence it
was a ballet of abstract form. (7)

———

Though I have abandoned [electric motors]
to some extent now, I still like the idea,
because you can produce a *positive* instead
of a fitful movement—though on
occasions I like that too. (6)

———

With a mechanical drive, you can control
the thing like the choreography in a ballet
and superimpose various movements: a great
number, even, by means of cams and other
mechanical devices. To combine one or two
simple movements with different periods,
however, really gives the finest effect,
because while simple, they are capable
of infinite combinations. (6)

—

I have made a number of things for the open air: all of them react to the wind, and are like a sailing vessel in that they react best to one kind of breeze. It is impossible to make a thing work with every kind of wind. (6)

———

There wasn't much metal around during the war years [in Roxbury], so I tried my hand at wood carving in the so-called constellations. I have always liked wood carving, but these were now completely abstract shapes. … They had a suggestion of some kind of cosmic nuclear gases—which I won't try to explain. I was interested in the extremely delicate, open composition. (20)

———

After some consultation with Sweeney
and Duchamp, who were living in New York,
I decided these objects were to be called
"constellations." (45)

———

In the constellations nothing moved,
and it was a very weird sensation I experi-
enced, looking at a show of mine
where nothing moved. (45)

———

Materials and Methods

There's no formula—but using your senses. (4)

———

When I use two circles of wire intersecting
at right angles, this to me is a sphere—and
when I use two or more sheets of metal cut
into shapes and mounted at angles to each
other, I feel that there is a solid form, perhaps
concave, perhaps convex, filling in the dihe-
dral angles between them. I do not have a
definite idea of what this would be like,
I merely sense it and occupy myself
with the shapes one actually sees. (10)

———

About my method of work: first it's the state
of mind. Elation. I only feel elation if I've
got ahold of something good. (12)

The lugubrious aspect [of Michelangelo's
Slaves] is eliminated in my approach to
sculpture. . . but the gay and the joyous,
when I can hit it right, are there. (12)

My fingers always seem busier
than my mind. (4)

You see nature and then you try
to emulate it. (13)

I like to work in any medium where
I am free to do as I choose. (30)

Wire, or something to twist, or tear, or bend,
is an easier medium for me to think in. (6)

It must be the twitching of my fingers—even
naked (without pliers), which makes me
want to be plastik! (4)

I enjoy walking in the streets looking at the
fences, the gray walls, the effects of light.
That's what I call living paint. (22)

———

I've made so many mobiles that I pretty well
know what I want to do, at least where the
smaller ones are concerned, but when I'm
seeking a new form, then I draw and make
little models out of sheet metal. (13)

———

Sometimes I make sketches for my mobiles.
But I can never know in advance what
I'm going to do. (23)

———

I used to begin with fairly complete drawings, but now I start by cutting out a lot of shapes. Next, I file them and smooth them off. Some I keep because they're pleasing or dynamic. Some are bits I just happen to find. Then I arrange them, like *papier collé*, on a table, and "paint" them—that is, arrange them, with wires between the pieces if it's to be a mobile, for the overall pattern. Finally I cut some more on them with my shears, calculating for balance this time. (12)

I feel that the artist should go about his work simply, with great respect for his materials. As the painter must be conversant with his colors, their pigments and vehicles, so as to produce something which is not contrary to the laws of chemistry, so the sculptor must have a feeling for the materials he uses, whatever it may be, and use it in accordance with its strength + nature. (29)

———

Simplicity of equipment, and an adventurous spirit of attacking the unfamiliar or unknown are more apt to result in a primitive, rather than decadent, art. And somehow the primitive is usually much stronger than that in which technique and flourish abound. (29)

———

Sculptors of all places + climates have used
what came readily to hand. They did not
search for exotic + precious materials. It was
their knowledge and invention which gave
value to the result of their labors. (29)

———

[Precious materials] never appealed to me.
A wood sphere painted vermilion is much
better than a gold one. (4)

———

I have always had a fondness for old bits
of iron (see <u>fork</u>), wire, cans, etc. Much like
Schwitters—Merzbild—"Merz" means
a reject, what is cast off. (I think Barr
suspected something else when
he showed Schwitters.) (4)

———

In 1928 when I started to carve wood, at
first I had "woodcarvers chisels," but soon
changed to carpenter's chisels because
I could hit them harder. (4)

———

A knowledge of, and sympathy with, the qualities of the materials used are essential to proper treatment. (9)

———

Stone, the most ancient, should be kept massive, not cut into ribbons. The strength must be retained. (9)

———

Wood has a grain which must be reckoned with. It can be slender in one direction only. (9)

———

[Wood's] strength in one direction is many times that in another. It should be dealt with so as to conserve this strength. (29)

———

Bronze, cast, serves well for slender, attenuated shapes. It is strong even when very slender. (9)

———

Wire, rods, sheet metal have strength, even in very attenuated forms, and respond quickly to whatever sort of work one may subject them to. (9)

———

The admission of approximation is necessary,
for one cannot hope to be absolute in his
precision. He cannot see, or even conceive of a
thing from all possible points of view, simul-
taneously. While he perfects the front, the side,
or rear may be weak; then while he strength-
ens the other facade he may be weakening that
originally the best. There is no end to this. To
finish the work he must approximate. (9)

It is even desirable that one face be
of finer quality than the others, for this
gives a head and a tail to the object
and makes it more alive. (9)

Disparity—in form, color, size, weight, motion—is what makes a composition, and if this is attained, then the number of elements can be very few. (29)

———

Symmetry and "order" do not make a composition. It is the <u>apparent</u> accident to regularity, which the artist controls, and with which he makes or mars the work. (29)

———

When I cut out my plates, I have two things in mind. I want them to be more alive, and I think about balance. Which explains the holes in the plates. The most important thing is that the mobile be able to catch the air. It has to be able to move. (23)

———

What I produce is not precisely what
I have in mind—but a sort of sketch,
a man-made approximation. (10)

———

Strength and durability in sculpture
are highly desirable. However, fineness
and delicacy may be even more essential
to the general concept, and it will then
be necessary to decide which is to
control the design. (9)

———

When I have used spheres and discs, I have intended that they should represent more than what they just are. More or less as the earth is a sphere, but also has some miles of gas about it, volcanoes upon it, and the moon making circles around it, and as the sun is a sphere— but also is a source of intense heat, the effect of which is felt at great distances. A ball of wood or a disc of metal is rather a dull object without this sense of something emanating from it. (10)

———

So I make a small maquette, in aluminum sheet metal, perhaps 50 cm high. With that I'm free to add a piece, or to cut some away. As soon as I am satisfied with the result I'm going to have, I bring the maquette to my Biémont friends (there are three of them, or even more!) and they enlarge my model as much as I want. When the enlargement is finished, more or less, I go there to add the ribs and gussets, or other things I had not thought of. After that they carry out my concept for the reinforcements.

And that's it. (18)

———

For me, increase in size—working full-scale in this way—is very interesting. I once saw a movie made in a marble quarry, and the delicacy of movement of the great masses of marble, imposed of necessity by their great weight, was very handsome. (6)

―――

I try something new each time. With the model at three meters you can wobble it and see where it gives, where the vibrations occur, and then put your reinforcement there. (24)

―――

If a plate seems flimsy, I put a rib on it,
and if the relation between the two plates is
not rigid, I put a gusset between them—that's
the triangular piece—and butt it to both
surfaces. How to construct them changes with
each piece; you invent the bracing as you go,
depending on the form of each object. (24)

———

There's been an *agrandissement* in my work.
As time goes on, I've developed new
mechanical devices, such as a bearing
that makes a swivel and fulcrum all in
one, to cause the object to rotate
and oscillate. (75)

———

Even in aluminum and very small,
at the model stage, the object must please
completely, whether it is intended to be
made in large dimensions, or not. (21)

———

The sculptures are often improved by
being related properly to site and scale. Once
I had to design one that crept up a circular
stairwell—a fascinating problem! (12)

———

I find that everything I do, if it is made for
a particular spot, is more successful. (13)

———

I don't use rectangles—they stop. You can
use them; I have at times but only
when I want to block, to
constipate movement. (13)

———

[Color is] really secondary. I want things
to be differentiated. Black and white are
first—then red is next—and then I get sort
of vague. It's really just for differentiation,
but I love red so much that I almost want
to paint everything red. I often wish
that I'd been a *fauve* in 1905. (13)

———

I have chiefly limited myself to the use of black and white as being the most disparate colors. Red is the color most opposed to both of these—and then, finally, the other primaries. The secondary colors and intermediate shades serve only to confuse and muddle the distinctness and clarity. (10)

———

To me the most important thing in composition is <u>disparity</u>. Thus black and white are the strong colors, with a spot of red to mark the other corner of a triangle which is by no means equilateral, isosceles, or right. To vary this still further use yellow, then, later, blue. Anything suggestive of symmetry is decidedly undesirable, except possibly where an approximate symmetry is used in a detail to enhance the inequality with the general scheme. (9)

I like to work alone. My wife never comes into the workshop, except in the evening to see what I have done during the day. I have always refused to work collectively. (21)

Sometimes I paint for three and four months at a time. I'd like to do more painting. But even in a big studio, like the one I have in America, the points of my mobiles threaten to puncture my canvases. (23)

———

Now and then you get out of your bailiwick and then you don't know what to do, so the best thing is to make drawings. (16)

———

On a few occasions, quite long ago, I have witnessed etchers rubbing and caressing their copper plates, with what might have almost passed for affection. But I have been content to spit on the plate, and then dump a little acid on it, and then watch the solvent and the dissolvent fume and bubble, all the while tickling the plate, and brushing away the bubbles, with a partridge feather. (65)

———

I prefer <u>daylight</u> in my shop because I want to see clearly what counts, and be able to eliminate in my mind what does not count. (4)

———

My sky is studded with about 150
screw eyes. (59)

———

[In Rio de Janeiro] things were arranged in
such a way that I could drag the workbench
into the garden and cut and hammer
in the sun. (60)

———

You do something and then you do
something else. One can never come
back to the same thing. (16)

[A found object] only works if you find something as good as the shape you were about to invent. I've used spoons as well as bits of bottles, but you can usually make something better, perhaps basing your design on what you've found. (12)

I have made things, such as mobiles and several fish, with pendent pieces of broken glass selected by me—some eroded by sea and sand, which I picked up on beaches. (49)

In 1943, aluminum was being all
used up in airplanes and becoming scarce.
I cut up my aluminum boat, which I had
made for the Roxbury pond, and I used it for
several objects. I also devised a new form of
art consisting of small bits of hardwood
carved into shapes and sometimes painted,
between which a definite relation was estab-
lished and maintained by fixing them
on the ends of steel wires. (45)

———

When I am at a loss for inspiration I think of what Sweeney, or Sartre, or perhaps one or two others, have written on my work and this makes me feel very happy, and I go to work with renewed enthusiasm. (14)

———

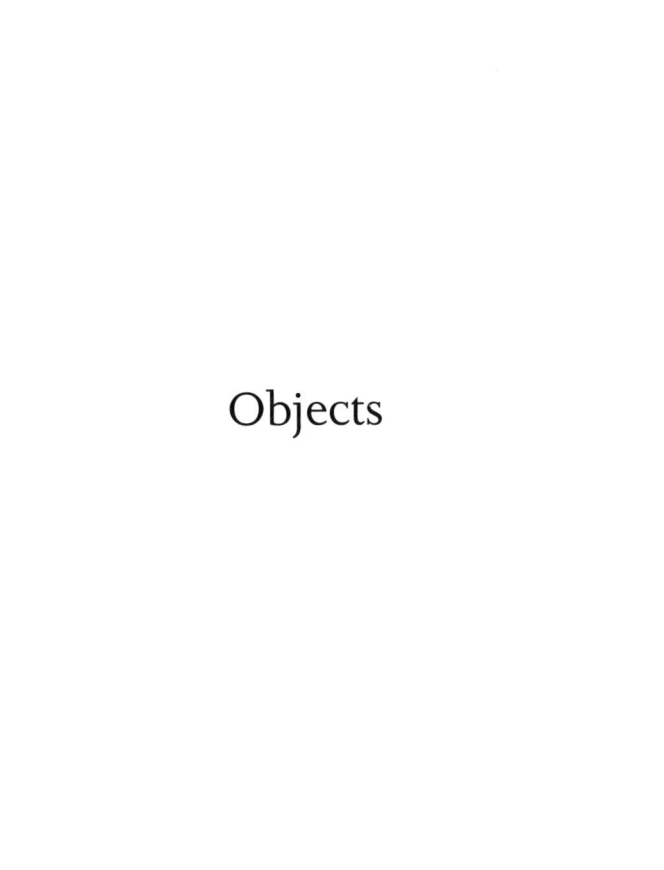

Objects

My mobiles are objects in space; I say
I'm a sculptor to avoid a fuss. What I want
to avoid is the impression of mud piled
up on the floor. (23)

———

For a couple of years in Paris I had a small
ballet-object, built on a table with pulleys at
the top of a frame. It was possible to move
colored discs across the rectangle, or fluttering
pennants, or cones; to make them dance, or
even have battles between them. Some of them
had large, simple, majestic movements;
others were small and agitated. (6)

———

I tried it also in the open air, swung between trees on ropes, and later Martha Graham and I projected a ballet on these lines. (6)

———

[*Double Arc and Sphere* and *Dancing Torpedo Shape*] are from among the more successful of my earliest attempts at plastic objects in motion. The orbits are all circular arcs or circles. The supports have been painted to disappear against a white background to leave nothing but the moving elements, their forms and colors, and their orbits, speeds and accelerations. (5)

———

In [my studio on] Villa Brune, I had tried
my hand at stone sculpture. ... One of the
things I had made was a horse; the legs were
in bas-relief around the solid base. On the rue
de la Colonie, we had no sidewalk and a
puddle always appeared right in front of the
entrance steps when it rained. So sometime in
the previous spring, I had buried my horse in
the pavement to plug up the water hole—not
being very enthusiastic about my sculpture.
Mary Reynolds and Marcel Duchamp had paid
a visit to Gabrielle Picabia and discovered the
horse in the sidewalk. They dug it up and took
it home, leaving me with the hole that
continued to catch the water, worse than
ever. They thought they had discovered
a Roman ruin. (50)

I made an abstract ballet using a frame
with rings in the 2 top corners through which
strings passed from the hands to the objects—
springs, discs, a weight with a little pennant...
—Varèse liked ballet (but not "music").
I called it "A Merry Can Ballet." (4)

———

Someone told me that Albert Einstein
once spent forty minutes in front of
[*A Universe*] figuring it out. (75)

———

I did a setting for Satie's *Socrate* [in 1936]. ...
The whole thing was very gentle, and
subservient to the music and the words. (6)

———

Possibly due to the Paris 1937 World's Fair, one day I went with my friend Miró to see the proposed Spanish pavilion where he was to do a large painting. I met José Luis Sert, the architect of the pavilion. When I saw what was going on in general in this pavilion, which included "Guernica" by Picasso, I promptly volunteered my services to do something or other for it. Sert was against this, for obviously I was no Spaniard, but later on, when he had received a fountain displaying mercury from Almadén, which looked like a plain drinking fountain, he called me in to get him out of the dilemma. (49)

———

[Mercury Fountain] proved quite a success, but a great deal was due, of course, to the curious quality of the mercury, whose density induced people to throw coins upon its surface, and often three hundred francs were taken in a day in this manner, for the benefit of the Spanish children. (77)

———

Léger was there and said to me: "Dans le temps tu étais le Roi du Fil de Fer, mais maintenant tu es le Père Mercure." (In the old days you were Wire King, now you are Father Mercury.) (51)

———

Some of the objects [1937 Mayor Gallery] were very slender and filmy—little lines of fine wire—and I used to turn out the light and project them on the wall with a flashlight as they turned around. (61)

———

How did you begin to use sound in your work? It was accidental at first. Then I made a sculpture called *Dogwood* with three heavy plates that gave off quite a clangor. Here was just another variation. You see, you have weight, form, size, color, motion and then you have noise. (13)

———

[Red Petals] was made during the war for
a little octagonal room lined with rosewood.
As I become professionally enraged when
I see dinky surroundings, I did my best to
make this object big and bold—to dwarf
these surroundings. (52)

As it was during the war, I went to a junkyard and bought a big chunk of an old boiler. It had a pebble grain due to the action of the water in the boiler, which gave it a very fancy surface. I cut out a big somewhat-leaf-shape [for *Red Petals*], which standing on end came to seven feet high, with an arm standing out at the top. This was held vertical by two leaf-shape legs behind it. From the arm overhead, I hung some red aluminum leaves—they might well have been remnants of the boat of the Roxbury pond. (52)

———

The first constellation I had made was a small thing to stand on a table, with at one end a small carved thing looking like a bone and painted red. At [Pierre] Matisse Gallery, this was standing on the floor and Jacqueline Breton, who was separated from André and affected an enormous Great Dane, came to the show with her mutt, and when he saw this bone-shaped object he menaced it and made as though to take a snap at it. (45)

———

[The 1944 bronzes] was rather an expensive venture and did not sell very well, so I abandoned it for my previous technique. It was also disagreeable to have to check the manipulations of some other person working on the objects at the foundry. However, I play with the idea, from time to time, of going back to this medium. (62)

—————

When I made *Double Helix* I did not know that it was going to become the basis of all genetics. (73)

—————

I got rather excited making [standing mobiles] as small as my so-called clumsy fingers could do them. Then in the fall of 1945, Marcel Duchamp said, "Yes, let's mail these little objects to Carré, in Paris, and have a show." So a whole race of objects that were collapsible and could be taken to pieces was born. (53)

———

When I had the show in Paris during 1946 at Louis Carré's gallery, the plans called for small sculptures that could be sent by mail. The size limit for things sent that way was $18 \times 10 \times 2$ inches, so I made mobiles that would fold up. Rods, plates, everything was made in two or three pieces and could be taken apart and folded in a little package. I sent drawings along showing how to reassemble the pieces. (13)

———

There were two mobiles of the epoch of the constellations—the war period—made of bits of hardwood, carved, painted, and hanging on strings at the end of dowel sticks. Carré had previously deleted these from what he wanted to show, so I gave them to Mary Reynolds, who was back in Paris. And she always refers to them, ever since, as the "Pas Nobles Mobiles" (the undignified mobiles). (53)

———

André Masson brought [Jean-Paul Sartre]
to see us in Roxbury and I saw him again
in New York, where he came to my little
shop. I gave him a mobile bird made out
of Connecticut license plates—there is
nothing tougher than these; they look like
aluminum, but they hang on forever. (53)

———

Henri Pichette ... wanted me to decorate
his new play: *Nucléa* [in 1952]. ... I was
interviewed by a journalist once and told him
I was learning the play "through osmosis,"
because I never did see a complete
copy of the text. (54)

———

In 1954 I'd done the *Water Ballet* for Eero
Saarinen's General Motors Technical Center
in Detroit. The concept there was a large one,
I'd say. Jets of water. Lines of water can
be monumental too. (24)

In the summer of 1955, Carlos Raúl Villan-
ueva, of Caracas, arranged a show for me. ... I
also saw him in 1952 in Paris. He had said
then that he was doing an auditorium and
wanted me to do something for the lobby, a
mobile. I said, "I'd rather be in the main hall."
And he said, "Oh! No! You can't do that
because the ceiling is taken up with ribbons
of acoustical reflectors." I said, "Let us play
with these acoustical reflectors." (55)

[The work] I like best is the acoustic ceiling in Caracas in the auditorium of the university. It's made from great panels of plywood— some thirty feet long—more or less horizontal and tilted to reflect sound. (13)

———

When I embarked on stabiles and heavier objects, following Noyes's purchase of "The Black Beast," I often worked in several metal shops at the same time. In 1958, I had three metal shops working for me, two in Waterbury and one, ten miles away, in Watertown. I got a sense of being a big businessman as I drove from one to another. (56)

———

In one shop, I was making the head of the object for UNESCO, "The Spiral"; in another shop, I was making the forty-five-foot mobile for Idlewild [Airport]; in Watertown, in the third, I was making "The Whirling Ear" for the Brussels Fair. It is still in Brussels, a gift of the United States. (56)

———

I also like the work I did for UNESCO in Paris and the mobile called *Little Blue under Red* that belongs to the Fogg [Museum]. That one develops hypocycloidal and epicycloidal curves. The main problem there was to keep all the parts light enough to work. (13)

———

When we went to the airport to put [Pittsburgh] up, they had all sorts of journalists standing around asking this, that and the other. I was trying to concentrate on getting the thing up. One of those guys asked me, "How long did it take you to make that?" I said, "Two or three months." Then I reconsidered and went back to him and said, "Hey, it took me thirty years." (24)

―――――

Your mobile in front of the UNESCO Palace, in the Place de Fontenoy, has caused something of a scandal. It will pass. The sculpture will remain. (22)

―――――

I made the model for [The City] out of scraps that were left over from a big mobile. I just happened to have these bits, so I stood them up and tried them here and there and then made a strap to hook them together—a little like *objets trouvés*. (13)

———

How do you feel about your motorized mobiles? The motorized ones are too painful—too many mechanical bugaboos. Even the best are apt to be mechanically repetitive. There's one thirty feet high in front of Stockholm's modern museum made after a model of mine. It has four elements, each operating on a separate motor. (13)

———

The biggest object [at Musée National d'Art Moderne in 1965] was "Deux Disques"—too big to put inside, so it was erected on the sidewalk by the entrance. Buses with visitors stopped and people got out to have their pictures taken in groups under the stabile; others took pictures of the object at various angles. As compared to the previous Guggenheim show, I liked the predominance of the big stabiles in the long hall, although there was no such effect as "The Ghost," hanging from the ice-cream cone, over the "Guillotine." (63)

———

[*The Ghost* was] bought by the Museum of Art in Philadelphia, where my grandfather had done the William Penn on the top of City Hall and my father had done the Logan Square fountain. So now they say that they have "the Father, the Son, and the Unholy Ghost." (57)

———

Hilla Rebay came to me and asked if I would make a mobile for the middle of the Guggenheim. I said I'd make a big black one. She said, "Mr. Wright wants you to make it out of gold." I said, "All right, I'll make it out of gold, but I'll paint it black." (24)

———

The title of [*Tamanoir*] was just some vague association. After I had finished it and walked around it, it began to look like an anteater. On this business of titles, sometimes it's the whole thing that suggests a title to me, sometimes it's just a detail. (67)

———

A title is just like the license plate on the back of a car. You use it to say which one you're talking about. (69)

———

I don't like that name [*Le Guichet*].
I only called it that to identify it. (70)

———

In the beginning I called it *Three Discs*, but
when I got over to Canada, they wanted to call
it *Man* as a sort of theme for the exposition. ...
When we first talked about a sculpture twenty
meters tall—that's about 64 feet—they asked
me to stretch it to 67 feet because it was
1967. But I told them that was like giving me
the commission because I was 67 years old.
I happened to be 67 then. (68)

———

It's called [*Monsieur Loyal*] because it's
between two recreation parks, between a
track and a recreation playground and a
modest school. In France, the name of the
circus ringmaster in any circus is Monsieur
Loyal, so we called it that because he's in
charge between the areas. It's black.
It's nine meters high—that's about
twenty-eight feet. (24)

———

For thirty years I have been thinking about
a production that would be entirely mine,
form and music working together. I long ago
discussed this with Massine, but he insisted on
having dancers. I later made stage sets, but this
is not exactly what I wanted to do. ... for
Satie's *Socrate*, Pichette's *Nucléa*, John Butler's
The Glory Folk in Spoleto, for Joe Lazzini in
Marseille. The idea of a production that was
totally mine had already come to me in
spirit in 1926 when I finished the *Cirque*,
and when I tried to frame it in a stage
opening, amusing myself by thinking
it an actual theatre. (71)

———

I should have called [*Work in Progress*]
"My life in nineteen minutes." (71)

———

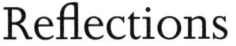

Reflections

As an artist I have always carried on my work without fear of comparison with existing and accepted art, having, rather, invited this. (And I think it must have been this possibility which lead me to take up art in the first place.) (66)

———

There is one thing, in particular, which connects [wire sculpture] with history. One of the canons of the futuristic painters, as propounded by Modigliani, was that objects behind other objects should not be lost to view, but should be shown through the others by making the latter transparent. The wire sculpture accomplishes this in a most decided manner. (1)

———

How can art be realized? Out of volumes, motion, spaces bounded by the great space, the universe. Out of different masses, light, heavy, middling—indicated by variations of size or color—directional lines—vectors which represent speeds, velocities, accelerations, forces, etc. ... —these directions making between them meaningful angles, and senses, together defining one big conclusion or many. (2)

———

Not extractions, but abstractions. Abstractions that are like nothing in life except in their manner of reacting. (2)

———

Fernand Léger's film, "Ballet Mécanique," is the result of the desire for a picture in motion. (5)

———

Marcel Duchamp's "Nude descending the stairs" is the result of the desire for motion. Here he has also eliminated representative form. This avoids the connotation of ideas which would interfere with the success of the main issue—the sense of movement. (5)

———

Why not plastic forms in motion? Not a simple translatory or rotary motion but several motions of different types, speeds and amplitudes composing to make a resultant whole. Just as one can compose colors, or forms, so one can compose motions. (5)

———

A "Mobile." Dimensions: 2 meters by 2 meters 50. Frame: 8 centimeters, neutral red. The 2 white balls turn very rapidly. The black helix turns less rapidly and seems to always climb. The iron plate turns still less quickly, the two black lines seeming always to climb. The black pendulum, 40 centimeters in diameter, climbs by 45° on each side, passing in front of the frame, at the rate of 25 turns a minute. (27)

———

The esthetic value of these objects cannot be arrived at by reasoning. Familiarization is necessary. (5)

———

The various objects of the universe may be constant, at times, but their reciprocal relationships always vary. (3)

———

There are environments that appear to remain fixed whilst there are small occurrences that take place at great speed across them. They appear so only because one sees nothing but the mobility of the small occurrences. (3)

———

There is the idea of an object floating—not supported—the use of a very long thread, or a long arm in cantilever as a means of support seems to best approximate this freedom from the earth. (10)

———

I think I am a realist ... [b]ecause I make what I see. It's only the problem of seeing it. If you can imagine a thing, conjure it up in space—then you can make it, and *tout de suite* you're a realist. The universe is real but you can't see it. You have to imagine it. Once you imagine it, you can be realistic about reproducing it. (13)

———

So it's not the obvious mechanized modern world
you're concerned with?
Oh, you mean cellophane and all that crap. (13)

———

It takes the edge off things, to discuss
them. (4)

———

The basis of everything for me is the
universe. The simplest forms in the universe
are the sphere and the circle. I represent them
by disks and then I vary them. My whole
theory about art is the disparity that exists
between form, masses and movement.
Even my triangles are spheres, but they
are spheres of a different shape. (13)

———

The underlying sense of form in my work has been the system of the Universe, or part thereof. For that is a rather large model to work from. What I mean is that the idea of detached bodies floating in space, of different sizes and densities, perhaps of different colors and temperatures, and surrounded and interlarded with wisps of gaseous condition, and some at rest, while others move in peculiar manners, seems to me the ideal source of form. (10)

———

I would have them deployed, some nearer together and some at immense distances. And great disparity among all the qualities of these bodies, and their motions as well. (10)

———

Spheres of different sizes, densities, colors and volumes, floating in space, surrounded by vivid clouds and tides, currents of air, viscosities and fragrances—in their utmost variety and disparity. (17)

———

Spaces, volumes, suggested by the smallest
means in contrast to their mass, or even
including them, juxtaposed, pierced by
vectors, crossed by speeds. Nothing
at all of this is fixed. (2)

———

The mechanical element must never
control the aesthetic. Much better a poor
machine and a good sculpture. (9)

———

The motors are not so good. I had my choice between perfecting a motor for one or two things or going on to new creations.
I preferred to go on creating. (28)

———

I don't think the engineering really has much to do with my work; it's merely the means of attaining an aesthetic end. (13)

———

Do you consider your work particularly American?
I got the first impulse for doing things my way in Paris, so I really can't say. (13)

———

Laziness is a product of leisure. You have
to know how to use your free time, which
is a good climate for invention. (23)

———

[I would prefer to live] in the Middle Ages.
That's what we lack in America, and what
I am searching for in France. (22)

———

I do like the dogwood tree, perhaps because
it has a shape. A shape to hang things on.
A rose has only the blush of youth.
No shape. (12)

———

I'm frank to say that in religious pictures what moves me is the plastic forms or the wonderful colors. Or in Bosch, who is antireligious, I suppose, the endless invention of forms and symbols. My friend Peter Blume wants to say something. I don't.

Who comes out best? (12)

What artists do you most admire?
Goya, Miró, Matisse, Bosch and Klee. (13)

The mobile has actual movement in itself, while the stabile is back at the old painting idea of implied movement. You have to walk around a stabile or through it—a mobile dances in front of you. (13)

———

My business is to create sculptures, static or mobile, life or not, and not to think about the noise and movement of the underground and the cars. This poses in priority the problem of the space reserved for these sculptures. Not the reverse problem. (21)

———

I feel that there's a greater scope for the imagination in work that can't be pinpointed to any specific emotion. That is the limitation of representational sculpture. You're often enclosed by the emotion, stopped. (12)

———

I believe that in modern work the spectator has to bring with him more than half the emotion. To most people who look at a mobile, it's no more than a series of flat objects that move. To a few, though, it may be poetry. (12)

———

In [handling the mobiles], i.e. setting
them in motion by a touch of the hand,
consideration should be had for the direction
in which the object is designed to move,
and for the inertia of the mass involved.
… gentle is the word. (9)

———

A mobile in motion leaves an invisible
wake behind it, or rather, each element leaves
an individual wake behind its individual
self. Sometimes these wakes are contracted
within each other, and sometimes
they are deployed. (9)

———

A sculpture in the town should be used like a sea or river navigation marker with its red discs, its squares and its black triangles. It should be designed as a real urban signal. (21)

———

The pigeon is rather a dumb animal, yet it has a handsome motion. To enjoy that motion, why must I tolerate an unpotted squab? (28)

———

So-called Industrial Design is not a fine art. Its motive is to instill "style," i.e. a yearly trend, be it up or be it down, in our daily commodities. (9)

———

I give a mobile a name the same as you
get a license plate for your car. It's just a ticket,
or identification, if you wish. I once started
using unusual tree names, but I soon
got bored with that. (31)

———

Didn't use to name [the mobiles] at all,
in the beginning. When I wanted to talk
about one of them, I'd have to draw it.
It was cumbersome. (76)

———

Although the army says that the painter is of little or no use in modern camouflage, I feel that this is not so, and that the camoufleur is still a painter, but on an <u>immense scale</u> (using color, materials, forms, plant life, etc. as his media), and in a <u>negative sense</u> (for instead of creating, he <u>demolishes</u> a picture, and reduces it to nil, to the best of his ability). (66)

A mobile is like a dog-catcher.
A dog-catcher of wind. (23)

Myself, I'm like my mobiles: when I walk in the streets I latch onto things, too. (23)

———

I like Chicago on the Michigan Avenue Bridge on a cold wintry night. There used to be no color but the traffic lights, occasional red lights among the white lights. I don't think that looking at American cities has really affected me. We went to India and I made some mobiles there; they look just like the others. (13)

———

When we crossed the Amazon River
[in 1948], the moon shone in spots from
overhead on the river and cut out great black
islands of different shapes; this was not
always very distinct, but when you could
grasp it, it was stunning. (64)

———

He who stops to reflect what others will
think of his work is lost, for anything
adventurous is bound to arouse
negative comment. (29)

———

People think monuments should come out of the ground, never out of the ceiling, but mobiles can be monumental too. (24)

———

How do you feel about your imitators?
They nauseate me. (13)

———

When an artist explains what he is doing he usually has to do one of two things: either scrap what he has explained, or make his subsequent work fit in with the explanation. (6)

———

I feel that if one accepts things which one does not approve of, it is the beginning of the end, and by and by you get more things of a similar nature. This is akin to the stunt of giving objects away which you don't like. Then the people think you do like that sort of thing, and pretty soon they'll give you back something of a similar nature. (41)

———

Bad taste always boomerangs. (41)

———

Theories may be all very well for the artist himself, but they shouldn't be broadcast to other people. (6)

———

I have developed an attitude of indifference to the reception of my work, which allows me to go about my business. (44)

———

That others grasp what I have in mind seems unessential, at least as long as they have something else in theirs. (10)

———

SOURCES

1. Calder, Alexander. Statement on Wire Sculpture. Manuscript, 1929. Calder Foundation archives.

2. Calder, Alexander. "Comment réaliser l'art?" *Abstraction-Création, Art Non Figuratif*, no. 1 (1932): 6.

3. Calder, Alexander. "Que ça bouge—À propos des sculptures mobiles." Manuscript, March 8, 1932. Calder Foundation archives.

4. Calder, Alexander. "The Evolution." Manuscript, 1955–56. Calder Foundation archives.

5. Calder, Alexander. "Statement." In *Modern Painting and Sculpture: Alexander Calder, George L. K. Morris, Calvert Coggeshall, Alma de Gersdorff Morgan*. Exhibition catalogue. Pittsfield, MA: Berkshire Museum, 1933.

6. Calder, Alexander. "Mobiles." In *The Painter's Object*, edited by Myfanwy Evans. London: Gerald Howe, 1937.

7. Calder, Alexander. Manuscript, 1956. Calder Foundation archives.

8. Calder, Alexander. "Statement." In *17 Mobiles by Alexander Calder*. Exhibition catalogue. Andover, MA: Addison Gallery of American Art, 1943.

9. Calder, Alexander. "À Propos of Measuring a Mobile" III. Manuscript, 1943. Agnes Rindge Claflin papers concerning

Alexander Calder, 1936–circa 1970s. Archives of American Art, Smithsonian Institution.

10. Calder, Alexander. "What Abstract Art Means to Me: Statements by Six American Artists." *Museum of Modern Art Bulletin* 18, no. 3 (Spring 1951): 8–9.

11. Calder, Alexander. "Voici une petite histoire de mon cirque." In *Permanence du Cirque*. Exhibition catalogue. Paris: Revue Neuf, 1952.

12. Rodman, Selden, ed. "Alexander Calder." In *Conversations with Artists*. New York: Devin-Adair, 1957.

13. Kuh, Katharine. "Alexander Calder." In *The Artist's Voice: Talks with Seventeen Artists*. New York: Harper & Row, 1962.

14. Calder, Alexander. "Statement." In *4 Masters Exhibition: Rodin, Brancusi, Gauguin, Calder*. Exhibition catalogue. New York: World House Galleries, 1957.

15. Oral history interview with Alexander Calder, October 26, 1971. Archives of American Art, Smithsonian Institution. https://www.aaa.si.edu/collections/interviews/oral-history-interview-alexander-calder-12226.

16. Gray, Cleve. "Calder's Circus." *Art in America* 52, no. 5 (October 1964): 20, 22–48.

17. Calder, Alexander. "Handwritten statement." In *Exposición Calder*. Exhibition catalogue. Caracas: Museo de Bellas Artes, 1955. In *Calder: Gravity and Grace*, edited by Carmen Giménez and Alexander S. C. Rower, 52. Exhibition catalogue. New York: Phaidon, 2004.

18. Calder, Alexander. "Comment faire." *Derrière le Miroir*, no. 141 (November 1963): 20. In *Calder: Sculpting Time*, edited by Carmen Giménez and Ana Mingot Comenge, 41. Exhibition catalogue. Milan: Silvana Editoriale, 2024.

19. Calder, Alexander. *Animal Sketching*. New York: Bridgman, 1926.

20. Calder, Alexander. Commentary for Constellations, 1943. In *Calder*, edited by H. H. Arnason and Ugo Mulas, 202. New York: Viking Press, 1971.

21. Bruzeau, Maurice. "Alexander Calder, a Blacksmith in the Town." *Revue Française des Télécomunications* (December 1973): 47–51.

22. Ustinov, Peter. "Je suis un bricoleur." *Arts, Lettres, Spectacles*, no. 687 (September 9–16, 1958). In *Calder: Gravity and Grace*, edited by Carmen Giménez and Alexander S. C. Rower, 87. Exhibition catalogue. New York: Phaidon, 2004.

23. Taillandier, Yvon. "Calder: Personne ne pense à moi quand on a un cheval à faire." *XX Siècle*, no. 2 (March 13, 1959): 5. In *Calder: Gravity and Grace*, edited by Carmen Giménez and Alexander S. C. Rower, 87–88. Exhibition catalogue. New York: Phaidon, 2004.

24. Osborn, Robert. "Calder's International Monuments." *Art in America* 57, no. 2 (March–April 1969): 32–49.

25. Osborn, Robert. "A Conversation with Alexander Calder." *Art in America* 57 (July–August 1969): 31.

26. "Futurist Toys for Advanced Kiddies Created by Calder,

Artist-Engineer." *New York Herald* (Paris Edition),
August 4, 1927, 7.

27. Calder, Alexander. "Un Mobile." *Abstraction-Création,
     Art Non Figuratif*, no. 2 (1933): 7.

28. "Objects to Art Being Static, So He Keeps It in
     Motion." *New York World-Telegram*, June 11, 1932.

29. Calder, Alexander. "À Propos of Measuring a
     Mobile" II. 1943. Manuscript, 1943. Agnes Rindge
     Claflin papers concerning Alexander Calder, 1936–
     circa 1970s. Archives of American Art, Smithsonian
     Institution.

30. Soby, James Thrall. *Calder, Matisse, Matta, Miró:
     Mural Scrolls*. New York: Katzenbach and Warren,
     1949.

31. Friedman, Shirley M. "Originator of 'Mobiles'
     Comments on This Art." *Newark Evening News*,
     July 28, 1954.

32. Calder, Alexander. "January 15, 1965." In *Calder: An
     Autobiography with Pictures*, edited by Jean Davidson,
     11–15. New York, Pantheon, 1966.

33. Calder, Alexander. "January 16, 1965." In *Calder:
     An Autobiography with Pictures*, 15–27.

34. Calder, Alexander. "January 19, 1965." In *Calder:
     An Autobiography with Pictures*, 36–42.

35. Calder, Alexander. "January 29, 1965." In *Calder:
     An Autobiography with Pictures*, 55–58.

36. Calder, Alexander. "January 30, 1965." In *Calder: An Autobiography with Pictures,* 58–72.

37. Calder, Alexander. "February 1, 1965." In *Calder: An Autobiography with Pictures,* 72–78.

38. Calder, Alexander. "February 3, 1965." In *Calder: An Autobiography with Pictures,* 82–91.

39. Calder, Alexander. "February 9, 1965." In *Calder: An Autobiography with Pictures,* 112–14.

40. Calder, Alexander. "January 28, 1965." In *Calder: An Autobiography with Pictures,* 53–55.

41. Calder, Alexander. "February 16, 1965." In *Calder: An Autobiography with Pictures,* 122–24.

42. Calder, Alexander. "February 17, 1965." In *Calder: An Autobiography with Pictures,* 125–27.

43. Calder, Alexander. "February 18, 1965." In *Calder: An Autobiography with Pictures,* 130–37.

44. Calder, Alexander. "February 25, 1965." In *Calder: An Autobiography with Pictures,* 147–49.

45. Calder, Alexander. "March 15, 1965." In *Calder: An Autobiography with Pictures,* 177–82.

46. Calder, Alexander. "January 18, 1965." In *Calder: An Autobiography with Pictures,* 31–36.

47. Calder, Alexander. "January 25, 1965." In *Calder: An Autobiography with Pictures,* 48–53.

48. Calder, Alexander. "February 2, 1965." In *Calder: An Autobiography with Pictures,* 78–82.

49. Calder, Alexander. "March 5, 1965." In *Calder: An Autobiography with Pictures*, 154–58.

50. Calder, Alexander. "February 23, 1965." In *Calder: An Autobiography with Pictures*, 141–42.

51. Calder, Alexander. "March 8, 1965." In *Calder: An Autobiography with Pictures*, 158–63.

52. Calder, Alexander. "March 18, 1965." In *Calder: An Autobiography with Pictures*, 185–87.

53. Calder, Alexander. "March 30, 1965." In *Calder: An Autobiography with Pictures*, 188–94.

54. Calder, Alexander. "April 6, 1965." In *Calder: An Autobiography with Pictures*, 208–12.

55. Calder, Alexander. "April 19, 1965." In *Calder: An Autobiography with Pictures*, 231–46.

56. Calder, Alexander. "April 22, 1965." In *Calder: An Autobiography with Pictures*, 249–58.

57. Calder, Alexander. "May 4, 1965." In *Calder: An Autobiography with Pictures*, 258–71.

58. Calder, Alexander. "February 7, 1965." In *Calder: An Autobiography with Pictures*, 106–8.

59. Calder, Alexander. "March 11, 1965." In *Calder: An Autobiography with Pictures*, 168–71.

60. Calder, Alexander. "April 2, 1965." In *Calder: An Autobiography with Pictures*, 200–202.

61. Calder, Alexander. "March 10, 1965." In *Calder: An Autobiography with Pictures*, 165–68.

62. Calder, Alexander. "March 31, 1965." In *Calder: An Autobiography with Pictures*, 194–98.

63. Calder, Alexander. "March 15, 1966." In *Calder: An Autobiography with Pictures*, 273–77.

64. Calder, Alexander. "April 1, 1965." In *Calder: An Autobiography with Pictures*, 198–200.

65. Calder, Alexander. "The Ides of Art: 14 Sculptors Write." *The Tiger's Eye* 1, no. 4 (June 15, 1948): 74.

66. Calder, Alexander. Application for the Marine Corps. Manuscript, September 21, 1942. Calder Foundation archives.

67. Calder, Alexander. Commentary for *Tamanoir*, 1963. In *Calder*, edited by H. H. Arnason and Ugo Mulas, 204. New York: Viking Press, 1971.

68. Calder, Alexander. Commentary for *Trois disques I*, 1967. In *Calder*, edited by H. H. Arnason and Ugo Mulas, 205. New York: Viking Press, 1971.

69. Kempton, Murray. "Mr. Calder Laughs." *New York World-Telegram & Sun*, November 16, 1965.

70. Glueck, Grace. "Ticket Window (Nonfunctional) Is Installed at Lincoln Center." *New York Times*, November 12, 1965, 49.

71. Carandente, Giovanni. "Work in Progress." In *Calder: Mostra retrospettiva*, 231–32. Exhibition catalogue. Turin: Palazzo a Vela, 1983.

72. Calder, Alexander. Commentary for *Croisière*, 1931. In *Calder*, edited by H. H. Arnason and Ugo Mulas, 202. New York: Viking Press, 1971.

73. Calder, Alexander. Commentary for *Dancer*, 1944. In *Calder*, edited by H. H. Arnason and Ugo Mulas, 203. New York: Viking Press, 1971.

74. Calder, Alexander. "Pourquoi j'habite Paris ..." *Nord-Sud* (March 1931).

75. Hellman, Geoffrey T. "Onward and Upward with the Arts: Calder Revisited." *New Yorker* (October 22, 1960): 25–30, 33.

76. Casey, Phil. "His Art Stumps Man of Motion." *Washington Post*, January 25, 1958, B1.

77. Calder, Alexander. "Mercury Fountain." *Stevens Indicator* 55, no. 3 (May 1938): 3, 7.

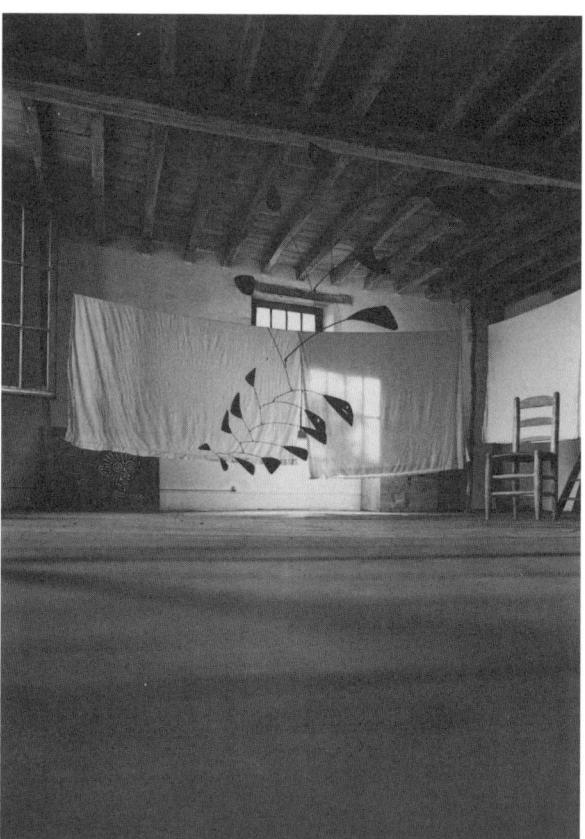

SELECTED CHRONOLOGY

*The Calder Foundation, New York, maintains an extensive chronology
   at www.calder.org*

1898
Alexander Calder is born in Lawnton, Pennsylvania,
   to Nanette Lederer Calder, a painter, and Alexander
   Stirling Calder, a sculptor.

1906–15
The Calder family moves often due to Stirling's
   commissions, living in Pasadena, California;
   Croton-on-Hudson and Spuyten Duyvil, New York;
   and San Francisco. From the age of eight, Calder is
   given a workshop in the cellar of the family home.

1915–19
Calder attends Stevens Institute of Technology, Hoboken,
   New Jersey, and graduates with a degree in mechani-
   cal engineering.

1922

Serving as a fireman in the boiler room, Calder sails
from New York to San Francisco on the passenger
ship H. F. *Alexander*, via the Panama Canal. Off the
coast of Guatemala, he is struck by the rising sun
and setting moon on opposite sides of the horizon.
Calder finds a job as a timekeeper for a logging camp
in Independence, Washington. Inspired by the
landscape, Calder writes home and asks his mother
for paints and brushes.

1923–25

Calder enrolls in classes at the Art Students League of
New York. He also begins his first job as an artist,
illustrating sporting events, city scenes, and the
circus for the *National Police Gazette*.

1926

Calder carves his first wood sculpture, *Very Flat Cat*, from
an oak fence post.
In his one-room apartment at 249 West Fourteenth

Street, he makes his first wire sculpture, a sundial in the form of a rooster.

Calder settles in Paris, where he enrolls in drawing classes at the Académie de la Grande Chaumière and establishes a studio at 22 rue Daguerre. He begins creating *Cirque Calder* (1926–31), a complex body of performance art made from a spectrum of found materials. He also makes his first formal wire sculptures, *Josephine Baker I* and *Struttin' His Stuff*.

1928

Weyhe Gallery, New York, presents *Wire Sculpture by Alexander Calder*, the artist's first solo show in the United States.

1929

Calder's first solo show of wood and wire works is held at Galerie Billiet-Pierre Vorms in Paris. Jules Pascin writes the preface to the catalogue.

Galerie Neumann-Nierendorf, Berlin, presents *Alexander Calder: Skulpturen aus Holz und aus Draht*.

Calder creates his first formal mechanized sculpture, *Goldfish Bowl*, and presents it to his mother as a Christmas gift.

1930

At 7 Villa Brune, Calder hosts a *Cirque Calder* performance for the international avant-garde, including Fernand Léger and Piet Mondrian. He later visits Mondrian's studio at 26 rue du Départ. Deeply impressed by the environment, he begins to work in the abstract.

1931

On January 17, Calder marries Louisa James in Concord, Massachusetts.

Calder's abstract work is presented for the first time in *Alexandre Calder: Volumes—Vecteurs—Densités / Dessins—Portraits* at Galerie Percier, Paris. Léger writes the introduction for the catalogue.

Marcel Duchamp visits Calder's 14 rue de la Colonie studio and sees his latest works. When Calder asks

Duchamp what to name the motorized objects, he
at once proposes "mobile" and arranges a show
for Calder at Galerie Vignon.

1932

Calder: ses mobiles is held at Galerie Vignon, Paris.
Soon after, his first show of mobiles in New York
is presented at Julien Levy Gallery.
In response to Duchamp's term "mobile," Jean Arp asks
sarcastically if the objects from the previous year
at Galerie Percier were "stabiles." Calder adopts the
term for his static objects.

1933

The Calders return from Europe and settle in Roxbury,
Connecticut. They purchase an eighteenth-century
farmhouse, and Calder converts the adjoining ice-
house into a modest dirt-floored studio. Five years
later, he builds a large studio on the foundation of
a burned-down dairy barn on the property.

1934

Mobiles by Alexander Calder is presented at the Pierre
Matisse Gallery, New York, the beginning of Calder's
nine-year relationship with the gallery.

1935

Mobiles by Alexander Calder is shown at the Renaissance
Society at the University of Chicago.
On April 20 the Calders' first daughter, Sandra, is born.
Calder constructs mobile sets for Martha Graham's dance
Panorama and begins working on "visual preludes"
for her dance *Horizons* (1936).

1936

Organized by Alfred H. Barr Jr., *Cubism and Abstract Art*
is presented at the Museum of Modern Art, New York.
Calder is represented by three works. Works by Calder
are also included in another MoMA exhibition,
Fantastic Art, Dada, Surrealism.

1937

Calder is commissioned to make *Mercury Fountain* by the architects of the Spanish Pavilion at the 1937 World's Fair in Paris.

1938

Calder's first retrospective, *Calder Mobiles*, is presented by the George Walter Vincent Smith Gallery, Springfield, Massachusetts.

1939

Calder is commissioned by the Museum of Modern Art to make the mobile *Lobster Trap and Fish Tail* for the principal stairwell of the museum's new building on West Fifty-Third Street.
On May 25, the Calders' second daughter, Mary, is born.

1942

Calder begins to work on a new open form of sculpture made of carved wood and wire. James Johnson Sweeney and Duchamp propose the name "constellations" for these works.

1943

The Museum of Modern Art presents *Alexander Calder: Sculptures and Constructions*, curated by Sweeney and Duchamp. Originally scheduled to close on November 28, 1943, the exhibition is extended to January 16, 1944, due to public demand.

1946

Alexander Calder: Mobiles, Stabiles, Constellations opens at Galerie Louis Carré, Paris. The catalogue includes an essay by Jean-Paul Sartre.

1948

Calder and Louisa arrive in Rio de Janeiro for the opening of *Alexander Calder* at the Ministerio da Educaçao e Saude. A solo show follows at Museu de Arte, São Paulo.

1949

Calder constructs his most ambitious mobile to date,

International Mobile, for the Third International
Exhibition of Sculpture, Philadelphia Museum
of Art.

1950
Galerie Maeght, Paris, presents *Calder: Mobiles and Stabiles*.
Massachusetts Institute of Technology, Cambridge,
    exhibits *Calder*, a retrospective.

1952
Calder designs the sets and costumes for *Nucléa*, a play
    written by Henri Pichette.
Calder represents the United States in the XXVI Biennale
    di Venezia. Calder wins the Grand Prize for sculpture.

1953
The Calders arrive in the hamlet of Les Granettes in
    Aix-en-Provence. At a blacksmith shop nearby, he
    makes a series of large standing mobiles conceived
    for the outdoors.
Calder agrees to a trade of three mobiles for François

Premier, a dilapidated seventeenth-century stone house in Saché that adjoins a cliff on the property of future son-in-law Jean Davidson. Over time, Calder acquires more land in Saché and builds a large studio and home.

Museu de Arte Moderna, São Paulo, presents the II *Bienal*. United States representation consists of three exhibitions, including a solo show of works by Calder.

1955

In Caracas, Calder sees for the first time his *Acoustic Ceiling* (1954), commissioned for Aula Magna at the Universidad Central de Venezuela.

1956

Calder completes his fountain commission, *Water Ballet*, for the General Motors Technical Center, Warren, Michigan.

1957

Calder finishes .125, a mobile commissioned by the

Port Authority of New York. It is installed in the International Arrivals Building of Idlewild Airport (now John F. Kennedy International Airport) upon the building's completion.

1958

Calder completes the motorized, monumental sculpture *The Whirling Ear*, a commission made for the pool in front of the United States Pavilion at the Brussels Universal and International Exhibition. He also installs *Spirale*, a monumental standing mobile commissioned for UNESCO in Paris.

1962

Calder agrees to a proposal to make a sculpture for the Spoleto Festival in Italy. He conceives *Teodelapio*, a colossal stabile arching the roadway near the town's train station.

Tate Gallery, London, exhibits *Alexander Calder: Sculpture—Mobiles*, a retrospective.

1964

Calder completes the large-scale standing mobile *Chef d'orchestre* for composer Earle Brown's *Calder Piece* (1963–66).

The Solomon R. Guggenheim Museum, New York, exhibits *Alexander Calder: A Retrospective Exhibition*.

1965

The Musée National d'Art Moderne, Paris, presents *Calder*, a retrospective.

As a member of Artists for SANE (Committee for a Sane Nuclear Policy), Calder participates in a march to protest against the Vietnam War in Washington, DC.

1966

On behalf of SANE, the Calders publish a full-page ad in *The New York Times*.

Calder donates *Object in Five Planes* (1965), a monumental stabile, to the United States Mission at the United Nations, New York, and dubs it *Peace*.

1967

Calder's *Trois disques* I, commissioned by the International Nickel Company, is presented at the 1967 International and Universal Exposition (Expo 67) in Canada.

1968

Calder's "ballet without dancers," *Work in Progress*, is performed by the Teatro dell'Opera, Rome.

In Mexico City, Calder views his *El Sol Rojo* at Aztec Stadium, commissioned for the Summer Olympic Games. The stabile stands more than eighty-four feet high.

1969

Fondation Maeght, Saint-Paul-de-Vence, France, exhibits *Calder*, a retrospective.

Calder attends the dedication ceremony for *La Grande vitesse*, commissioned for the city of Grand Rapids, Michigan, and the first sculpture funded by the public art program of the National Endowment for the Arts (NEA).

1973

Braniff International Airways launches Calder's *Flying Colors*, a painted DC-8 jet. Two years later, Calder paints a Boeing 727, *Flying Colors of the United States* (1975), commissioned by Braniff in honor of the bicentennial.

1974

Prompted by Calder's project with Braniff International Airways, French auctioneer and race car driver Hervé Poulain commissions Calder to design the first-ever BMW Art Car, which upon its completion competes in the 1975 24 Hours of Le Mans.

Calder accepts the Commandeur de la Légion d'Honneur of France. He also receives the Grand Prix National des Arts et des Lettres.

1976

The Whitney Museum of American Art, New York, presents *Calder's Universe*, a major retrospective. The exhibition travels to fifteen cities throughout the United States and Japan.

President Gerald Ford offers the Medal of Freedom to
Calder. The artist declines in protest of the harsh
treatment of conscientious objectors.
On November 11, Calder dies in New York City at
the home of his daughter Mary.

ACKNOWLEDGMENTS

To Alexander Calder, whose words are the lifeblood of this book, my deepest gratitude. It is a privilege to contribute to such an extraordinary legacy.

My heartfelt thanks to Alexander S. C. Rower, Susan Braeuer Dam, Lily Lyons, Beryl Gilothwest, and the entire team at the Calder Foundation. Your unwavering dedication and thorough archival work were crucial to the realization of this publication.

My sincere appreciation, as always, to the entire team at Princeton University Press, especially Michelle Komie, Christie Henry, Terri O'Prey, Cathy Slovensky, Jacqueline Poirier, Colleen Suljic, Laurie Schlesinger, Cathy Felgar, Jodi Price, Kathryn Stevens, Annie Miller, William Skurka, and Alexandria Leonard. Your professionalism and passion have been instrumental in bringing our projects to life over the years.

My thanks as well to Robert Rubin for his valued contributions to the cultural history of Alexander Calder, and many more.

Special appreciation goes to editorial director Fiona Graham for her leadership in guiding this project and the entire ISMs series. My thanks also goes to Susan Delson for her insightful editorial input, and to Vanessa Lee for her early research contributions.

My sincere thanks as well to Taliesin Thomas and Steven Rodríguez for their continued support.

Above all, I give all my bottomless gratitude to my amazing wife, Abbey, and to my wonderful children, Justin, Ethan, Ellie, and Jonah for their love and encouragement.

As always, I give endless love and thanks to my mother, Judith.

LARRY WARSH
MARCH 2025

Alexander Calder (1898–1976) utilized his innovative genius to profoundly change the course of modern art. Born in a family of celebrated, though more classically trained, artists, he began by developing a new method of sculpting: by bending and twisting wire, he essentially "drew" three-dimensional figures in space. He is renowned for the invention of the mobile, whose suspended, abstract elements move and balance in changing harmony. Coined by Marcel Duchamp in 1931, the word mobile refers to both "motion" and "motive" in French. Many of the earliest mobiles moved by motors, although these mechanics were virtually abandoned as Calder developed mobiles that responded to air currents, light, humidity, and human interaction. He also created stationary abstract works that Jean Arp dubbed stabiles.

From the 1950s onward, Calder increasingly turned his attention to international projects and monumental sculptures in bolted steel plate. Notable commissions include .125 (1957) for the New York Port Authority, John F. Kennedy Airport; *Spirale* (1958) for UNESCO, Paris; *Teodelapio* (1962) for Spoleto, Italy; *Trois disques I* (1967) for Expo 67, Montreal; *El Sol Rojo* (1968) for the 1968 Olympics, Mexico City; *La Grande vitesse* (1969) for Grand Rapids, Michigan; and *Flamingo* (1973) for the General Services Administration, Chicago.

Major lifetime retrospectives were held at the George Walter Vincent Smith Gallery, Springfield (1938); The Museum of Modern Art, New York (1943–44); Solomon R. Guggenheim Museum, New York (1964–65); The Museum of Fine Arts, Houston (1964); Musée National d'Art Moderne, Paris (1965); Fondation Maeght, Saint-Paul-de-Vence (1969); and the Whitney Museum of American Art, New York (1976–77).

Larry Warsh has been active in the art world for more than thirty years as a publisher and artist-collaborator. An early collector of Keith Haring and Jean-Michel Basquiat, Warsh was a lead organizer for the exhibition *Basquiat: The Unknown Notebooks*, which debuted at the Brooklyn Museum, New York, in 2015, and later traveled to several American museums. He has loaned artworks by Haring and Basquiat from his collection to numerous exhibitions worldwide, and he served as a curatorial consultant on *Keith Haring | Jean-Michel Basquiat: Crossing Lines* for the NGV. The founder of *Museums Magazine*, Warsh has been involved in many publishing projects and is the editor of the ISMs series and several other titles published by Princeton University Press, including Jean-Michel Basquiat's *The Notebooks* (2017), *Keith Haring: 31 Subway Drawings* (2021), and two books by Ai Weiwei, *Humanity* (2018) and *Weiweiisms* (2012). Warsh has served on the board of the Getty Museum Photographs Council and was a founding member of the Basquiat Authentication Committee until its dissolution in 2012.

ILLUSTRATIONS

Cover: Calder ink drawing, 1967.

Frontispiece: Calder in his Roxbury studio, 1950.
Photograph by Herbert Matter © Calder Foundation,
New York.

Page 136: Alexander Calder, *Black Mobile with Hole*, 1954.
Moulin Vert, Saché, ca. 1963. © Calder Foundation,
New York / Artists Rights Society (ARS), New York.
Photograph by Ugo Mulas © Ugo Mulas Heirs.

ISMs

Larry Warsh, Series Editor

The ISMs series distills the voices of an exciting range of visual artists and designers into captivating, beautifully made books of quotations for a new generation of readers. In turn passionate, inspiring, humorous, witty, and challenging, these collections offer powerful statements on topics ranging from contemporary culture, politics, and race, to creativity, humanity, and the role of art in the world. Books in this series are edited by Larry Warsh and published by Princeton University Press in association with No More Rulers.

Calder-isms, Alexander Calder

Obrist-isms, Hans Ulrich Obrist

Ono-isms, Yoko Ono

Minter-isms, Marilyn Minter

Fairey-isms, Shepard Fairey

Abramović-isms, Marina Abramović